In Loving Memory of
my Father, whom I miss tremendously,
Michael Brian Dennis Dean O'Brian Moriarty
1946–2020

THREADBARE

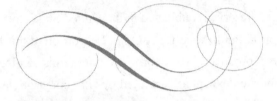

A Patchwork of Poems that Make a Life

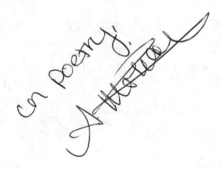

ADANNA MORIARTY

Threadbare by Adanna Moriarty

Published by Curious Corvid Publishing, LLC.

Cover design by Margherita Caprotti
Interior Design by Donna Loyd

Printed in the United States of America

Cataloging-in-Publication Data is on file with the Library of Congress.
ISBN: 978-1-7376916-7-9
ISBN (ebook): 978-1-7376916-8-6

www.curiouscorvidpublishing.com

For my mom, my husband, and my kids—I love you.
Thank you for always supporting me, even if the dream
seems crazy.

Pre-death
A precognition
I grieved you slightly—vastly
Knowing
Before you ever were gone.

Contents

The 'oos – The Mother

Dad

The '20s – Enter the Crone

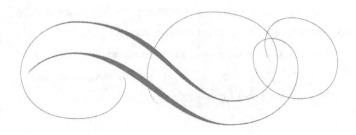

Acknowledgments

This book couldn't have happened without Community Literature Initiative (CLI). What I gained during their publishing course and how my writing, the way I think about it, and my voice have changed throughout this process is a testament to CLI and what they give poets to succeed. Without the guidance, education, and encouragement of Tommy Domino, I am 100 percent sure this book would never have left my closeted writing space.

Brenda Vaca, who became a steadfast friend throughout this process, troubleshooting with me outside of regular workshopping moments, encouraged me, checked on me, and inspired me with her beautiful poems.

I have to give honorable mention to my entire family who has borne with me, through thick and thin, manic joyful moments and the worst, dreaded "I'm not a writer" moments. I honestly couldn't have accomplished this book without them. My daughter, for just being a light in my life and willing to bring me food or grocery shop or come break up the monotony of editing to watch TV with me. My mother, for liking every single posted poem I put up, even when I thought it was crap. She generally thinks I am great and talented, and it's always so encouraging. My husband, who has read endless poems and looked at me and said, "I can't edit poetry!" but read it anyways, has asked me almost every day if this is a good writer's day or a bad one and adjusted accordingly—you're a champ, babe, I love you.

To every poet out there, thank you for gracing this world with your words, your voice, your inner demons, and the beauty that you are. Reading your work, social media posts of snippets, and journals that post prompts, and listening to your slams, spoken word poems, and open mics have been a constant inspiration to me when I was stuck. Thank you for always helping me create new pieces. This book is a dedication to your work as well because without it, I'd be stuck at twenty pages.

To my CLI(que), our Saturday morning church, this body of work has grown because of you. Your critiques during workshop helped me figure out where I was going. Your pieces, your strength, and your dedication to your work kept me moving forward during our time together. This has been no small feat for any of us. I'm honored to have gotten to know each of you and shared this journey with you all. Thank you, and I can't wait for your books—love and light to you all.

A special thanks to:

My editor: Kolby Baumgaertner

My cover designer: Margherita Caprotti

My interior layout designer: Donna Loyd

Sorrow comes in great waves...but rolls over us, and though it may almost smother us, it leaves us. And we know that if it is strong, we are stronger, inasmuch as it passes and we remain."

Henry James

Preface

I am here to tell a story, my story, your story, the stories that are told to me.

I am here to put ink to paper and write, fingers to keys.

I am here to show purpose through vocabulary.

I am here to shine my light page after page. Even if the darkness squeaks past the beams.

I am here to remember, as history repeats, over and over, personally, and worldly. I am here to capture that, in word.

Like Irish monks who worked day in and day out to save the world its stories. While the rest of the world burned them. I am here to scribe tirelessly and remember.

On most days I have yet to find my voice, but I am here to search under every rock until it sings to me, for you.

There is fear in this journey of writer/author, but I am here to overcome it.

I am not here to fail.

I am not here to buckle under my own weighted pressure.

I am not here to balk in the face of my path. Which is now so frighteningly clear.

I am not here to give in and give up on what I have always assumed was a child's folly.

I was put here to write, my story, your story, our stories.

With each poem, let my voice, our voice rise from the dark, and be the morning star to brighten the world around us.

Enjoy...

The '80s – The Child

My dad mowing the lawn at the house where this poem takes place, 1981.

I learned how to fly against my will

Twigs and sticks
flick in the mist
like dead fires
burning in the mouths of demons

And the careless wolves go out for moonlit walks

Barefoot feet
that tiptoe through the forest
alone
as not to make a sound

Footprints, one dainty and light
one with claws pressed deep.

Empty dens
abandoned until the spring
with fledglings pushed out
to learn to fly
whether they want to or not

Dark and scary corners
with manifested dreams
that die
in branches as the leaves fall.
I edged myself
pressed against walls

to slink in the dark
past scary monsters that dwelled in closets
and trolls perched on bookshelves

Running cautiously through swamps
as not to wake the mischievous and terrible goblins
that liked to grab my feet and try to make me one of them.

I laid the golden goose in tufts of
green earth
in stream beds
in hopes of treasure

Climbing to the tower of
the monkey bar castle
as my brother

Set the house afire
with paper airplanes, in the corpses of leaves

And I screamed at the dead burning fires
in the mouth of demons in the dark

As I took my room
in single bounds
so the creatures beneath my bed would stay
resting eternally
ignoring my very existence
Like everyone else

You see
we were raised by negligent wolves
and monsters hid in every shadowed corner

Every flower's bending darkness.

The fae spoke to me
and made me trade them bits and imaginary bobbles
for them to make the loneliness dissipate

And the wolves went to parties
ate fancy food
they weren't afraid
of the dark or the light
or the monsters that crouched in every bending dark place

the older cubs
tossed me around
like a ragdoll
misplaced in an epic
Dungeons and Dragons game.

Every sunrise
I escaped
to the world of fairy folk,
knights,
monsters, and demons
tippy toeing
through a haunted forest swamp

to freedom or my doom.

As my body changed and shifted
curved and bloomed

It became covered in feathers
I knew

I was not a Wolf
but a Bird

and I'd never fit anywhere
I'd never fit anywhere

So, I left my pack of wolves
and learned how to fly against my will.

Drowned

I saved myself
not when I drowned
the first time
when I was five
sand buckets held high
waving in frantic frenzy
as I sank to the rocky creek bed

not as I percolated
and the river's current washed away
my lifeforce
not as sunlight flicked
to stars

my brother's hand grabbed me then

But when I drowned again
I was twelve
I swam
gulped
grasped at each
particle of air

the ocean, angry I was there
she churned
violent
trying to swallow me whole
tear me to pieces

her power shoved me to the core of the earth

as my toes pushed off the heat
up through the other side
my face breaking the plane of one
world to the other
in those first, small
purposeful
still and quiet breaths
I saved myself

The Paris exploration of a nine-year-old

Even at nine
I can remember
the history that
pulsed in my feet
through the cobblestones

the Seine rushing by
muddy and fast
wondering, how they built
walls barricading its
flow, to something controlled, not wild.

We left my grandparents' apartment
every morning, to sit at the cafe across the street
I ordered endless croque monsieurs
an Orangina, to wash the richness down my throat
can you eat too many of them?
it's still what I dream of, when Paris comes to mind.

My mom had bought me
a red-and-white striped dress, made of cotton
I draped myself,
feeling especially Parisian
with leather, basket-woven shoes.

Walking history
unbroken leather shoes, forming blisters

consoled with red striped twirls
through ancient architecture, art,
spanning the centuries

the Louvre,
Rodin's garden, the Thinker sitting tall
The biggest man I'd ever met
Nutella crepe-packed mouths
from street vendors
women sunbathing naked off the banks
of Notre Dame.

How strange, yet amazing
people brought their dogs
to fancy restaurants!

I'd kick my shoes off under the table
while I ate bread smeared with butter
gorging on Paris in bites.

There was a love here
at nine, it grew deep within me
appreciation for architecture
food, the extravagance of gold-
lined ceilings.

I have never forgotten
the gleaming copper roof of
Napoleon's Tomb, that soared high enough to see

from the tiny balcony
nestled off my grandparents' apartment.

I have spent a life
searching, only to find
it's been impossible to replicate
how a Parisian croque monsieur made me feel.

The Dairy Queen Counter

glistens brown, in
soft yellow lighting
my fists, balled up

I look back anxiously
hoping there are forests in here
for me to hide in
the gentle textile of leaves.

But, it's just fluorescent lights
tables packed with boys
baseball uniforms, grass-stained

expectantly
a teenager looks down,
I gawk at the menu
open my mouth
a gust of wind flies out.

Where are the wolves?
I look around
anxiously
lips tingling
belly growling.

There was some purpose
for me to do this
alone, on my own

A hotdog, an ice cream
double-dipped in cherry
a Mr. Misty

My mouth dries from the back
I try again, mouth opening
it stays, clamped shut
my meekness digging
deep into my palm flesh.

A line grows behind me…

Overall buckles jangling
purple Converse
kicking carpet.

I walk away
belly growling.

Is hair who I am?

My mom never straightened my hair. I'd scream,
waller, and wail. She didn't like to brush it
either, she'd say, "You don't do this
for your sister?"

because my sister brushed it from the ends
up wet, gently so it didn't pull
and break.

The wallering and wailing
had my mom scheduling to cut it
short, like my brother's.

"What a cute little boy," strangers would say
at the diner on Sunday.

My short, curly hair, wild. My brother's hand-me-downs
covering, head to toe down to
his old, red striped sneakers.

I wallered and wailed until my mom bought me pink
bows, ribbons, and headbands,

I planted the bows in my hair, right up front
hoping the people wouldn't call me
"boy."

Wishing, at the diner on Sunday, someone would notice.
No one ever did. The bows got buried by the short,

bushy, wild.
bows devoured.

The Jewish grandmother's guilt always tried to
brush it, set it, make it
tame.

The proper slur is
Jew 'fro.

I envied the girls with straight hair, cute
little haircuts, the styles
they could shine.

at thirteen my mom deemed me capable
of brushing my hair,
I grew it as long
as I could.

hid the rat's nest at my nape, hoping
she wouldn't notice.

I hated the boy's haircut and the lady
who cut it, she threatened to slice
my ear off, when I couldn't sit still.

I rarely cut it now. When I do, I always grow
it back as fast as it will let me.

I've never hated or loved,
my hair.

"Your hair is beautiful," strangers, as they reach
for it. I try to dodge unknown fingers outstretched,
hopes of raking through
the mass on my head

Gracious deflecting, but
less than accepting, "Oh, I had a good wash day"
"This is day four," "Pssht, it's wild today,
must be humid"

Jew 'fro, I think, tucking it into my hoodie
wondering, is hair who I am?

Waller

Verb. The word originated from farmers who used the term to describe the pigs
"wallering" in the mud and their own shit.

Me and my sister Marisa at Latigo Beach in Malibu, California, early '80s.

*Me, in my brother's clothes, and our new puppy, Alice, in Ghent,
New York, early '80s.*

LA and Phoenix smell the same

every house and street,

maybe it's because my

grandparents lived in both

desert dwellers, who carried the

scent of life and dust with them

wherever they went.

Or maybe it was familiar because

they moved and I followed them

like the lost cactus searching

for water so it could bloom

prickly in the heat, enveloped

in the aromatic vapor of

chlorine and fabric softener.

Maybe it has nothing to do with

them, but instead the grubby cities

that loom around ticky tacky

boxed houses, lining streets

as far as every aerial view

can capture, pool water evaporating

into the air, creating a

lingering stench, wrapped around
every hair, gossamer to every soul.

LA and Phoenix smell the same,
an astringent home
hiding, burying the dirt and grime
that imbeds your fingernails, until
washed down bright white porcelain drains, only for

a sensitive kid, to build giant walls
with, their sameness
ensconced in the barrier of dirt
and grime, pavement and chlorine.

Not brave enough, to search out
the delicate cracks, where dandelions
bloom through impossible odds
but needing water, and fertilizer to creep
along the walls, lanking out on spindly
variegated vines, in search of
sun, in an endless downpour.

LA and Phoenix smell the same
there's something about memory

something comforting, but also pieces
that don't quite fit

maybe it's because my grandparents lived there
maybe it's how they carried the dust and life,
in their belongings, nomads, in a way
traveling back and forth, tracing
desert steps, searching for their granddaughter

only to be met with giant, saguaros walls
that hide a sensitive kid, writing
about dandelions instead
of picking them.

I am a soul to dive deep into
a river breaking through my ribs
a leaking vessel repaired
rebuilt by mud daubers
on false spring breezes
snow plunges in
thirsty mouths
hydrate
life

Plunge

The '90s – The Maiden

To the Nile with love—a homecoming

Scrungy kids
spanging for change
'hawks, liberty spikes
and deviated septum piercings
line the alley.

Waiting to get in
it doesn't matter who's playing
the floor will be sticky
and sweat will slide past you
as the whole room
moves in an amphibious
symbiotic relationship.

The music will pulse through
touching our souls
as stranger and friend become
one with you and then
the floor will shine
in the darkened space,

unsure if you're breathing
or everyone is breathing for you.

Each one,
one with the next
there's no divides here

it's home for each of us
as grommets get handed intoxicating
elixirs, from the ancestors of our tribe
and shirts and shoes are lost
to the abyss of the
Nile floor.

There's always someone crying acid tears
close to the speakers
as the pit vibrates out to the crowd
the street, the entire universe, can feel us.

We scream
fists pumping in the air
bodies slam in a wave
sardines with a single heartbeat
it's circular
infinite connectedness
no skin to define us.

The bathrooms have no sexes
they're sticky too
no soap or towels
it's all just one body,

amorphized on stage
as drumbeats get passed
surfing on the crowd
jumping from the rafters

the ultimate trust fall.

Walls drip with elated
vomited need
of each other's
joy
release.

We never knew we needed you so much
that we'd feel empty without each other,

when the lights come up
we're forced in a school of fish
through doors too small for who we became.

You can't be out of place here
you can't be left to twist
it's like, all that home
should have ever felt like
a violent love
spilled from cup and nose
and wounded hearts.

Spange
Spare Changing, formerly known as **Panhandling**. *It is a common practice amidst* **North American** *Homeless. Usually accomplished by «flyin' a sign," another common tactic beyond directly requesting financial assistance.*

NILE THEATER

105 W. MAIN MESA 649-2766
ALL SHOWS ALL AGES BAR W/ID
ADVANCE TIX AT FUGITIVE, EASTSIDE, STINKWEEDS, CDX, POLITICS, PRECINCT, AND HEADQUARTERS

Not everything that roams the earth is living

I died when I was seventeen
dirty streets and
dirty needles.

Dealers talk of throwing
people in dumpsters
when they OD.

I didn't die.
but I felt it.

As my skin was pierced
I could feel the water running in my eyes,
like static on the TV,
stuck within my throat
and bewitched came out my mouth,
tasting of classic TV shows,
fallen back on dirty motel beds

I died when I was seventeen.
In ecstasy.
Bottom lip biting
Toe curling
Awful bliss.

Dusty desert grime stuck
between my fingertips

I drew, I wrote,
and drank under bridges

purgatory didn't seem so bad.
 no
But there were no flowers here
only dusky city streets
dirty needles
jugs of wine.

I rode trains
to nowhere
only to end where I began,

Twilight streets
that burned barefoot feet
and dirty needles
In the city streets

I died when I was seventeen.

And purgatory seemed too long,
that's when I realized,

Not everything that roams the earth is living…

Trichinosis

I am sweat
I toss, turn,
wrap sheets through legs
dream of fitful days ahead,
for my underweight body.

I am chemical track marks
as the only shorts I own
seep into a stranger's bed.

I am static in my head,
I wonder,
is it permanent?

I am a tangled mess
of curly hair,
slicked to my neck.

Strange music pours
from beyond closed doors

I am locked,
reliant on people's
black hole faces,
dumped on a doorstep

I think of trichinosis
from the cat I share
this room with
I am whiteness
an abyss

I share with no one

I am each vibration
each turn of green light, red

a city pulses outside, alive

I am detox
with grime stuck
to me, like rage from
a needle

Boring through each level
of my addiction

I am taxed
broke
stripped to the teddy bear
and what I wear

I am homeless
lost in a phoenix's heat
leaking up through
chemical sweat

A fretful dream
once offered bliss
toss, turn
sleep while waking
toss, turn

I am thirst
in a needed glass of water

edged to a forced
feeding of cleanliness

Days of rigid liquidity
lost in surreal
moments of clarity

Waiting, for the tiny
glittering package of crystalline
that replenishes
A soul's deepest need,
it never comes.

I am time
weeks, hours, minutes
slick by, like silicone slips.
I leave this strangeness,
step into summer's full,
radiant, unmerciful inferno
burning, barefoot.

I am the clink
of the hollow dime
in a pay phone
searching for a connection.

Waiting for synapses
firing in a repaired
circuit board,
a cleanly, smoldering brain

I am the cleanness
of spring rivers

that flood a city
in monsoon rains.

Adrift, a starving body
finding meals
outside of the chemical mainline.

Trichinosis *is a foodborne disease caused by a microscopic parasite called Trichinella. People can get this disease by eating raw or undercooked meat from animals infected with the parasite. Often these infected meats come from wild game, such as bear or pork products, but it can also be spread through animal feces. This is a direct pop culture nod to 1996's* **Trainspotting***, where the character Tommy, a heroin addict, contracts trichinosis from his kittens—these two events, the situation of the poem and the movie, happened at the same time.*

If love was war

It's the start of the river
bubbles from the earth
squeaking between
rocks, birthing itself forward

that's love, clean and pure.

It's blood-soaked fields
the death of rivers
oceans can't sweep it away on the tides

That's war, battle ready and strong.

It's pure and bright,
like rain in the summer
love tangles the stalks of grass together
while dewdrops sparkle
in moonlight, glistening red

nothing is up, nothing
is down, because
if love was war

we'd not know the difference
our hearts patter out of
our chests, our skin is slick
our lips go numb.

If love was war
we'd still flatten ourselves
against walls
to hide what we've become.

That tough, soaked battlefield
glistens in tangled
moonlight
could be left by either

A ravaged love soaked
left weak in the knees,
or the clear and bubbling
river of young soldiers
who bleed into their lovers,
like riptide torn oceans
who only rise
to meet the moon
where rivers start.

If love was war, we'd
feed it with
our unholy bodies
spilling forth
onto the beaches left by moonlight.

These wars can only
be fought in the dark
while our souls dance heavy in armor
waiting for battle cries
that are love-soaked, pure.

Cast-offs

Thank you
I say to everyone
but it's a cast-off

autopiloted response
from an apathetic
no "thank you"
kind of place.

I get them back
"thank you's," "please's,"
"excuse me ma'am's."

I nod, saying
"thank you"
But, it's all a cast-off of

societal norms,
we walk, dazed
without seeing each other.

I no longer hear,
I float through tired
tired of a cast-off reply
to your cast-off introduction
to a society where apathy grows
and grows
and grows

It's like a slot machine winning,
"thank you's" cascade
from doors, windows,
steps, and rocks,

pings off concrete, tree,
flowers tilt their heads
squealing, "thank you, thank you"
as I step over them.

It's all just cast-offs
of societal norms
like dust,
pieces of trash that float through streets
in a more beautiful serenade
than the stalking
cast-off platitudes.

Chirping like the Game Boy
from the guy sitting next to me
on the train,

it's apathy bread
from that "nah, nope, not a thank you"
but a "fuck you" kind of place.

Forever in the mist

I am the dreamer.

The achiever.

The observer.

The outsider.

The non-conformist / Who must conform.

The believer.

The unbalanced / Who balances others.

I am the savior.

The healer / The advice giver.

Outside looking in.

Apart even when together.

Behind even when forward.

I am the misunderstood.

The one in the mist.

The loner.

The soul griever.

The observer.

The achiever.

The believer / The dreamer.

I am the outsider.

Me in the parking lot of a bar in Prescott, Arizona, 2000.

I lived for months without shoes,

hot, dusty sidewalks
piggybacking across pavement
that could cook bacon
in a minute.

Dumpster dives
into train rides
sweating the grime from skin
in place of showers
that could clean the bridges
and home-bums from
leather blackened spiky skin

Spit from strangers
the dimes in my pocket
that purchased generic cigarettes
food stamp change
that filled half a McDonald's hamburger
gorging on the only meal I'd see

Squat houses
bled acid to the streets
that urchin's matted hair roamed
punk rock shows
German army fatigues
sticky floors
salve to my sandblasted soles

A picture of '90s Phoenix
rising from the tap-dancing ashes

of a dirt city
filled with liberty 'hawks
squawking from the dust storms
that surrounded the A on the hill

The 602 sprawling
from a hole in the wall
beer runs on bicycles
stolen Cadillacs with gold-plated keys
left on freeways
to be eaten by the next monsoons
Couch surfing
squat chasing
Taco Bell bean burrito eating
teenager
standing on the edge of skateboard bowls
looking for my Simple shoes

Longing for the liniment
to save my bacon soles.

Life blooms from the desert

The last time I felt at home
was in the desert,
where the hot red earth,
swallowed me whole.
Held me in the center of its beating ventricles.
It held space for me,
amongst the dust,
and the prickly cactus.
An inhospitable landscape,
blooming in spring,
breathing life into me,
breathing for me
warming me from the core of the earth.
Teaching me,
life can come from drought.
Life can be warm,
and full,
even where no life should dwell.
Showing me life springs forward,
endlessly
hopefully
beautifully.
The last time I felt home,
I was swallowed by the earth
feeling its endless heartbeat.
The desert holds its breath with you.
Lets it out in a sigh of hot, dusty wind.
Then, the rains come.
Rolling from afar.
Drenching the red dirt.
Cleansing all that lies within its torrent.

Washing away every tear. Every heartache, every piece of pain.
Leaving you to stand.
On a lonely piece of earth.
Full
Full of everything.
Full of beauty
Full of hope
Full of life
Full of love
Full of warmth.
Full
Full of everything.

Me and Tess, Moab, Utah, 1998.

...To the end of time or the beginning

I have always been alone,
rooms to capacity,
brimming with the smells
of people who surround me.

A loneliness that encompasses
each inhale,
every flick of muscle
that propels me forward.

It's always been this way,
little zygotes swimming in puddles,
huddled together,
stepping onto flower-covered land,
stretching their Neanderthal legs.

Walking across the earth,
out of the valley of life,
hunting,
gathering,
farming,
into the industrial age.

I was left
sitting in Eden,
to watch
with an apple and a snake.

My tears stream
the mouth of rivers,
filling the oceans and lakes.

Calls unanswered,
flash floods
wept from my eyes,
unnoticed.

I have watched humanity
spread around me,
on their own search,

and one by one
dead,
like swatted flies.

From the zygote,
to the end of time,
I continued to sit, watching.

Now I walk upon the dead earth,
wondering if I had ever screamed,
would there at least be flowers
keeping me company?

Why are dewdrops frozen icy in
early moments? Are they waiting
to be birthed into spring's flood?
Melting deluge, lava
not molten, but cold
water racing
forward, like
melted
stone.

DewDrop

An unstoppable grace, unconstrained
by labor pains of winter, when
moving swiftly, only for
summer's bending heat, which
can evaporate
the flooding plain
that stills the
dewdrops'
breath.

The '00s – The Mother

Vermilion

bleeds into my soul, cascades

around me,

like a strange, euphoric

dream.

Heat pulses up through my feet,

and at last, I know

I'm free.

I have gone without

Often,
put food in another's mouth
with no thought for my own.

I have filled water
glasses,
while mine sits dry
lips cracked from thirst.

Given handfuls of
change,
while my bills sit
stamped, past due.

I have seen my
lights
flicker off, even while
I've given my last,

so another can live
without
darkness.

Why do others
not
live, and share
themselves like this?

I have gone without
often
lived poor, unsure
of where I'll sleep,

where my next meal
would
be graced from.
Dumpster, or soup kitchen?

I still go without,
not
often, but still
in those moments,

I think of
dried
Ramen packets, uncooked
the meals those bricks provide.

Belly rumbles, thirsty lips.
I've fought to provide
so the lights don't flicker.

Yet, I will empty
my
pockets for you
stranger, friend, lover
in need, without much thought

Why do others
not
live, and share
themselves like this?

Why do others
not
live, and share
themselves like me?

I wish I hadn't known

that love ache
that creeps in
through each part
of me.

I wish I hadn't known
what it felt like to miss this
feel of skin pressed to bone.

When your hands grabbed my
soul from my ribcage.

I wish I hadn't known
the loneliness I felt
when you slipped past me,
a ghostly whisper
in my ear.

If maybe on days,
and long nights
that were lost to
a jail of magnitudes
I could have never known.

I wish I hadn't known
what sitting in a room
felt like without you.
While girls giggle in the corner
and boys get drunk
from ice cube trays
at every party.

Because that's all that grows here.

Ice without you
and your tropical heat to thaw me
from places I didn't
know were cold.

I wish I hadn't known
before,

before I could hold onto you,
like that last tree
in a hurricane of wind,
that rips me from
my place,

and tosses me out like Dorothy
in her red shiny shoes.

Because, if I hadn't known,
my other love affairs
would have sung differently,
each its own serenade.

Instead of stealing kisses
in dreamscapes,
feeling your hands
on my curves,

when they ran their bodies,
over mine.
my eyes closed,
whispering your name,
that only I could hear.

If I hadn't known
I would have birthed more
children freely from my womb's
toxic environment,

but my body saved itself
for you, instead,
pulling you back through galaxies
that only your soul
could navigate back to

the heart that beat in my chest.

Our fingers danced
back together
in small, incubated moments
like they'd never
been separated.

If I had never known,
that our chest beats at once,
from paralleled universes,
my skin wouldn't have rippled
in darkened rooms calling you
home to me.

I am so tired

tired of not being heard.
tired of my body always moving
never being fed.

Tired of my mind
always being occupied
yet, always being blank
like my pen is out of ink.

Tired of decisions,
the weight they bear
my shoulders, always supporting.

Tired of responsibility
when all I want is freedom's release
to hide as far from here
with my feet dug into hot sand.

Tired of feeling wasted
never having space to fix my own
emotional well-being.

Tired of what this shit show
of a year has taken from me,
but here it is
taking more tired from me.

My tiredness...
My tiredness has broken my intuition...
My tiredness has stolen every moment of joy...
My tiredness has bankrupted my desire to eat...

My tiredness has corrupted my art…
My tiredness has canceled my empathy…
My tiredness has darkened my light…
My tiredness has tried to consume my goals…

Yet they dream…

My goals, they dream
sometimes without me.

My dreams are big.
My dreams push back against my pain.
My dreams hold space for my tiredness.

My dreams sing when I cannot.
My dreams keep writing even when
writer's block takes my hands from me.
My dreams find cracks in the pavement to grow,
even when I have wilted,
My dreams find air in the vacuum
even as I suffocate.

My dreams, are beautiful…

My dreams they swim the ocean
when I am drowning.
My dreams never quit,
because even my tired
can't smother their power to survive.

My daughter, two years old, down by the creek, Driggs, Idaho, 2004.

Winter 2002.

All that I was

became you
as my milk let down
to nourish your pure, tiny mouth

A love growing
my skin stretched tight around
tiger stripes protecting
perfect, tiny toes

The greatest love
squeezed from the most sacred parts
head frosted in sunlight
ocean-deep blue blinking
in sleepy newness

A growing foundation
spread around you
willing your curiosity
exploring how each pine needle drops
each river rock smoothed in time

Door's crack
for me to watch you grow
angelic face in sleep
painting my world in color
each dawning sunrise

Lightening to the shallows
of Caribbean blue
time starts to be told
in freckles dancing across the bridge

All that I was became you
my roots becoming your branches
a perch to allow observation
of the world
marking it in chalks and ink
a paint that only you can see

The greatest love
swelled from womb
to you, my daughter
Each day that's risen
Each bird song in spring
Each honeyed bee
Each fallen leaf
is my whisper of love
is my whispered strength
is my heart beating for you

I wish I had roots

locked in dirt
for generations
carrying that history on my shoulders.

Strong and tall
my branches stretched out
to the sun, soaking up rain
soil stabilizing my foundation.

I wish I had roots
where others knew me
watched me grow
seen my children flower.

Where storms have weathered my land
and my ancestors
battled rattlesnakes
survived droughts and famine.

I wish I had roots
a key the flowers misplaced
long ago,
an existence no one can remember
even the locks have been lost too.

I dream of the stability
I think of all the places I've lived
how they fit like a too-tight shoe
the soil, never settling around me.

I dream of tendrils
tied deep, gnarled and ancient
the tales they could tell
the honey the branches held for me.

I wish I had roots
that trickle to the ends of acres
supporting creature, river, and houses
where my mother, and hers, fingers weathered,

from the food they grew
that nourished my depths
as my branches lifted up
shading the delicate green fields that spread from me.

I dream of roots
searching endlessly, as time
slicks by, my tendrils spread out
over land and sea, always searching
never finding
home.

My body is the promised land

I never thought
of what she could do
the magnitudes of scars
that she overcame.

When she was little
knees scraped, bruises marking
each branch climbed to nestle
in the crook of leaves.

When she was small
legs took off across acres
of corn and swampland,
like lightning through
each blade of grass.

When she wasn't so small
each curve started to show
through fabric made, just
for her.

As she became bigger
she hid each arc of breastbone and hip
in folds of textiles
not designed for her
but others, larger

She thought, have I,
always been this way?
She hid in shirts,
tree branches, and swampland
slinking away, in hopes
that no one could reach for her.

Ashamed of every skinny
curve, that pressed
against threadbare fabric
unformed to her.

When she was grown
she took missing pieces
searching for the promised land
closely held, to make her whole again.

Some fit for a time, and
always wanted to stay
some she kept, but others
she set free, in rivers,
oceans, and lakes.

Some pieces
skipped and came back
others sank away.

Once she grew so big
another person came from her.

In all this time
she was adrift
never feeling comfortable
in the skin her bones wore.

Her shell, never being hers
what she thought was, again.

In all these moments
triumphs of being made
and unmade
she grew to be, in time,
more accepting of the casing
she bore.

The skin others wished to covet.

As she grew old
the slivers of silver, that
began to show the wear of time
looked back, nostalgic.

Until, one day, she looked upon me
green eyes bold, reflected face beaming,
arms wide, declaring, my body, your body,
THIS BODY
is the PROMISED land.

The Fabric that Makes Me

Everything of me
is threadbare
you can see the light through
the thinning of my fabric.

The house of me
is made of sorrow
it leaks from the floorboards
like tear ducts of a foundation.

The school of me
is knowledge that's seeped
from scar
that pretends to be skin.

A skin that has weathered
the storms that
tatter the fabric
that made it feel whole.

A fabric that felt
worthy of the knowledge it
gained, while building
the house that held it.

Everything of me
is threadbare
an emotion that has
no name to withhold it.

The house of me

is made of so much grief
it stands stark on a hill
with no trees to bear witness.

The lessons learned from
the school of me
are words to work through
to describe them.

The tatters flap
in the breeze
like a reminder of a flag
that once blocked the sun,

in recollection of vocabulary
that housed the densest
of fabrics.

The threadbare of me
takes the fray
and weaves them together.

For knowledge, and sorrow
melancholy and scar become
the patchwork of a rebuilt
foundation,

that supports the new me
cocooned in the woods
where the threadbare fabric becomes
integral, and the trees can
protect it.

NEOWISE, caught on my iPhone, kind of.

Dreams

I fall like NEOWISE
wakeful dreams
with trailing light
through darkened skies.

The Milky Way river,
dusty and clear
wraps round us
holding our soul to earth.

Light pollution
muddled and bright
colliding reality
blocking consciousness.

The mountains encompass
every star twinkles
the dark moon's light,
holding our breath like gravity.

Planets dance upon us
our blood ejecting to the cosmos,
Andromeda waits
with bateless sighs.

Shooting light
heavens waken,
galaxies spread wide
we come home in a nebula.

It's easy for the birds

in spring, they flutter and toil
foraging for sticks,
and bits of brightly colored yarn
fabricating a home, with beak and claw.

Fluttering in, out, in, out
only to abandon when the fall comes
babies free
blooming into their own
with adolescent spring.

As ancestors flee to Valhalla
fledglings pounce, collecting bright, shiny yarn,
manufacturing, nesting
among the Midgardian life.

My nest is empty
shades of gray
stillness encompasses it,
solitude
not even the wind twitches its branches.

There's a great void inside
A chasm that screams out,
hollow, dark, echoing
Niflheim

dead leaves, the blooming flower,
the emptiest of nests
I am the ghost, not you...
It's easy for the birds.

Working-Man's Hands

His hands slide over me
like sandpaper to the finest
grained wood.

A rough and uneven skin
scratching as it passes, over curve of
hip, dip in
rib bones.

I don't mind
I've never minded
his polishing,

reminding
with each prickly pass
a rough cat's tongue
the endeavors that go into making
those hands.

the strength behind each
uneven pass,

each scar,
each crack,
earned for us.

To trace each delicate finger bone
the sinew of forearm
bulge in bicep
absence of fat through chest and rib cage.

Each tracing step a reminder
of what those arms do for us
every task that shapes them

I've never minded
each sandpaper pass
as his hands slip, over curve of hip
breast and rib.

I've never minded
the yin and yang
the softness of me
the roughness of him,

we unfold for each other.

Silver Strand, Oxnard, California, 2012.

Anxiety rages inside

A storm
destroying the villages of my brain.

Injustice abounds
controlling every thought,
we're rife with deplorables
it's consuming me.

I'm hungry for action
hungry for change
I'm starving
starving for Eden.

Stagnant in anxiety
dumbfounded in anger
I am blocked,
unable to understand.

I've come to the quiet
I'm banging on abandoned doors
screaming to be heard.

It eats the depths of me
anxious housing
nobody seems to see
nobody seems to care,

We were searching for Eden.

My breath

is the only breath.
The sound of nature,
the only sound.

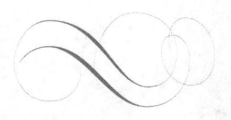

DAD

Sunburn

Don't let the clouds trick you
or the sun will burn you more
in whatever you are searching for.

That burning light shines through
setting my skin ablaze
that pain I needed,
to remind me
I'm not dying too.

Thunderclaps inside me
a forever brewing storm
I start wildfires
in a cloudless sunlit sky.

I can't escape this
it's like cancer wrapped
all throughout my soul.

Lava, molten hot, leaks
from every pore
I can't escape this
sunburnt blaze within my core.

I dare you, Earth,

To take me, raw, broken,
for my tears create your oceans.

I have pain for you to swallow me whole with.

I have love to be ejected into the stratosphere, like volcanic lava
from the depths of you.

I have this vapidness to be set adrift and carried out to sea from
your raging rivers spidering out across you.

I have a child that dwells, deep inside, who needs your forests to
envelop her, to be knitted into the strength of your roots.

I have rage, to be breathed into the wind, cocooned in the frozen
glaciers that hold the ancients.

I have sadness for the great sandstorms to radiate across the
desert, magnifying the heat, smothering everything in its path.

I dare you, Earth
To take me this raw, this broken, this bitter.

I dare you, Earth, to take me,
swathe my soul in your womb and let me rain back down with
hurricane force until I have sucked your oceans dry again.

I dare...

Only then can I be healed

Where do books come from?

Do I feel like this forever now? // do I cry forever now? // Is this
fleeting? // or is it all encompassing? // Are these the moments,
where "one foot in front of the other" comes from? // "pull
yourself up by your bootstraps"? // How do we go forward? //
Lost in waves of grief? // forever?

Hold tight to the ones you love // we are fragile vessels. // what
feels like an endless length of time // is short, a blink. // this is
where poetry comes from // where else can we bleed? // but from
inkwell to page.

Backstage, a Rabble concert, The Whisky, 1980.

August 2, 2020
You died today

You died today...
And just like that, we, go on
without you…
you became our ancestor
your stories became our history
your dreams, became ours.

You died today
and we, go on
without you…
your songs became our soundtrack,
the places that you touched
became, our holy ground.

You died today
and we, go on
without you…
your blood is our blood
for generations to come.

You died today
and our fragile vessels
go on
in our children
and yours.

You died today
and we, go on…

A history of me

I no longer know who I am.
Not who I "am"
but who I was.

It's an ebb and flow,
from waxing to waning,
like,
the tide being pushed as far as it can go
the lowest it will be,
straining from the highest it had ever been.

The history of us
the loss of you
the history of me?

My soul became the ocean
yours, a trip to the cosmos joining the
wisdom of our ancestors.

A magnitude of loss
a mourning of the greatest unknown?
The greatest I have ever known?

A vast and deep
Mariana trench
that sucks my history into
its dark abysmal depth.

I'll find myself
one day
and how I belong in a world
that's lost you.

Rose Mallows, Idaho August 2010

A meadow's grief

I need a meadow in a forest
where the wildflowers glisten
like stars in the dew
the thunder clouds roll overhead, and I lie there
thinking of the lightning that was in you.

I have put you in a box, and decided to honor you instead.
I can't grieve the loss of you.

There is stillness in the trees, even now
the storm brews in the chatter all around me.

I need the rushing of the river,
the stillness in the lake,
to find that spark of me, that ignited
from you.

I want to wall myself in stones
that come from rocky cliffs
watch the fires burn, as they snuff out all
my grief

I can't grieve the loss of you.

But my hands outstretched
looking for rope, I'm drowning,
so, I grieve you
anyway.

Take care of yourself
Take care of yourself

I have become a canyon
You can count the years between my layers.

The river of my ancestor has
shaped me,
the desert wind has smoothed my edges
only to be disrupted by the
flash of floods that spring forth from
my unknown depths.

My caverns scream
to my ancestor, in the darkest of
the moons, wishing the seeds of the
future could hear.

Take care of yourself
Take care of yourself

How to explain that unquenchable sadness

I feel milky with emotion
thicker than water, but liquid, nonetheless.
like an opaqueness that covers my whole essence
swimming in it, leaking from every orifice.

Blurring me, sucking me under
leaving me in a mucusy sludge.
I can almost breathe
but I cough with the coating in my throat.
It leaks silently,
dripping down my face as I fold towels,
answer the phone,
go about the things that make a life.

It's slippery and lonely,
and yet I'm still here,
all of it, at once.

I just want to be
hugged, embraced.
A moment of life to be set aside.
The milky feeling swells out into others,
and I am invisible.
My needs go under the surface,
unable to be seen through the opaqueness.

My stomach rolls in the lactose.
It's an unanswerable feeling,
unexplainable.
New, this milkiness I have
become.

Like I've drunk myself,
then washed the cup and
put it back. All I am is gone,
as the glass sparkles in the dish drainer.

Tetonia, Idaho, August 2020.

The Weight of Light

The August lawn sticks in my feet. It pokes and prods my soul.

The weight of you sits on my shoulders, pressing me deeper into the slanted light.

The pain urges me to stand still. But there is urgency in my toes.

Move forward they say. Let the pain rise up, but keep moving they say.

There is a wastefulness in this stagnated burden. There are things to accomplish. Move forward they say.

But to move, to let the sticks and prickles climb through my feet, requires a release of weight.

A release of you. It's not what he'd want, they say. There is joy to be found, they whisper.

Be barefoot longer, the soul will toughen. Toughen and move forward they say, there's comfort buried in the burden, they whisper.

Fissured

Tears snuck in today
held tight behind the damn I've built.

It's tall now, connected
with the grayest of skies
the wind can't touch me here.

Today is your birthday
the damn fissured
how could it not?

It's heavy behind the walls
pushing and pulling
with the might of the Titans.

A constant violent storm
battering the flesh it's made of,

I'm trying to sew the cracks, but
they break free with each
new stitch.

A damn isn't meant to hold this much
the weight behind it is wild
I have had to build the wall so tall
I cannot see the mountains.

A joint birthday party for my dad (center) and the woman getting cake shoved into her mouth, my mother is right behind her, the Whisky, midnight September 18, 1980.

The rhythm of frozen time

I don't want to fall into a rhythm
and forget...
forget that, I'm supposed to
miss you.

I want to forget that time moves forward,

time spans endlessly right now,
a week becomes a day
a single month,
in what used to be an hour.

There's a fear of the stars falling
all at once, in
bedlam deafening my
every second.

But while time stood still
each one fell around me, silent
laboring, each one gathered,

I packaged up the
shiny memories
tied them in tiny bows.

One day, I'll hang them
each from the moon's glow,
when time moves forward once again,

I'll take each package
pluck them out of frozen time,
hang each twinkling light
from deep within my memory.

I'll miss you then.
When I remember, time moves forward once again.

My Dad, in his rockin' star boots, sometime in the 1970s.

The '20s – Enter the Crone

Fuck you, 2020- and other thoughts of gratitude

New Year's Eve
we clean, put away
the year we've lived
with action
purpose.

I don't feel different, I feel
heavy, weighted
more so, than
yesterday.

I hope tomorrow
brings, elation
fortitude,

that collectively
we kick this dumpster fire.
We burn our wishes
and spread a new light

in the darkest months
a new year
brings a mystified magic
that source and universe

will firework us
to something better
and the weight shifts
as we creep closer

to a mythical flip in the page
whether it be New Year's
or just, tomorrow
always springs forth new
for us.

It's like a snow globe

falling snow, so gentle
It silences

Each tree branch bends
but never breaks
as the weight of it all
catches on each pine needle

They bear it for me
with whispers
of
I'm strong enough
for you

I watch them
silently
laying on my bed
through the window

The mountains behind swell
the inches turn to feet

while they hold it for me
with whispers
of
I'm built for this
for you

I hide in here
as the cloudy sky
magnifies the white
everything becomes the same

The space heater whirs
with whispers
of
I'll warm you

I sit on the bed
trying to find purpose
waiting
for the snow globe
to be shaken

The bed
with
whispers of
I'm here for you
I'll sleep for you.

I have withdrawn into myself

I feel the power of the earth swell up around me

I feel heavy, mystical and heathen at once

planets shift all around

I feel the weight of change

electrified in the air all around

consuming me

deafening and silent

a dissonance of human vigilance

pain

anxiety

strength and will

sickness, sadness

boredom and need

this crack

fissure...

Where does it take us,

who will we be tomorrow?

As I shift and grow

flower and bloom

I see my neighbors shift and fall

like dead leaves pulverized, dusty

back to days of things that were.

Days that should be behind us.

Yet they strengthen

take hold.

Like weeds in concrete

overtaking all that was building
cracking a foundation
of blood and freedom.

Who will you be tomorrow?
Who will I be?
Will we follow a progressive dream?
Will we slide further into darkened hate and malice?

As spring tides are born
a shift from self
a land awakening
hoping the dandelion blooms
weave their way
to unifying the fissures
healing a broken congregation.

How have You not died yet?

along with the demons who founded You?
how do You grow
flourish, even when

each new seed that springs up
tries with all their might to
sow their beauty all around You?

Your un-weeded roots
hold fast to the fabric that You came from
knitted in blotchy patches
through the delicate craftsman embroidery
that shaped You

Yet the dissent that
You think shaped You
lives deeper
in the pockets
that control Us

In the pockets that hold Us
In the pockets that control Us

How have You not died yet?

While the seeds sprung forth
in the fields that make You
shine in rainbow colors

sharing their beauty all throughout You

For centuries that each ancient color has spread around You

You hold tight, an uncomfortable homespun
A dullness thrown tightly round You
that's itchy for the rest of Us

The feet that march across You
can't soften
the very un-craftsmanship
You show Us

You hide from the silken colors
woven from the seeds that sprung You

A knitted craftsmanship that survives You
their seedlings take hold
and will flourish despite You.

In darkness of

winter months
I reach
stretch toward sun
fingertips extend
beyond body
capturing light

life sleeps
hibernating
sun, holy
each beam like god
gifting life

Sunbeams sing
false divine
my fingers stretching
stretching
from darkened shoulder
dusky elbow
gloaming fingernails

Capturing heat
like cat, in windowsill
snow covers beyond
reflecting false light

Encapsulating
waiting

summer-warmed fields
bare feet
shed of sock and shoe

Soaking
basking
long days' heat

I reach
stretch toward sun
fingertips extend
beyond body
capturing life

Gloaming: *A poetic word for "twilight," or the time of day immediately after the sun sets, is gloaming. The best thing about summer evenings is looking for twinkling fireflies in the gloaming.*
Also in the gloaming: when everything is in such perfect light it looks to be kissed by god.

I hear your voices

of change
screaming in majority

I feel the oppression
not as my own
but as yours
it burns me deeply
profoundly
to my soul

but who am I to even try to be an ally?

Who am I
for you to know
that you can grab my hand?
That I will never pull away

or shy from my responsibility to use my privileged voice

I'd burn bridges,
cities to the ground
for you to live safe like me

I lived off simple things

of forest floors and mushroom fairy rings
I gathered and grew
healing for each and every one of you

You'd come to me
in hopes of love potions
devised like poems to catch that man
that just keeps walking through

But your sister and her lover
came to me,
to fill her womb with wee bairns
I served you all
the best I could, until
the day

That preacher came
all each and every one of you could do
was scream
"Witch, Witch, Witch"

Then set a pyre, doused with the darkest
inky, sticky oil
you tried to strap me tight, set me
all ablaze

But I sang words of freedom's lullaby
watched you each fall in
deepest sleep

As you snored the smokey haze
I shucked my bonds
escaping to the
darkest moon

My power becoming
my daughter's daughters'
generations of light
to sing the songs, illuminating the blood
of our blood
hands to forest floors and mushroom fairy rings
living off simple things, healing each and
every one of you

This phone sucks the creativity
from my marrow
you're this or that on Facebook
this endless Instagram story

free moments
it's there
sucking away life
warm bodies
stare at their phones in every silenced second
every commercial break
every bathroom moment

zombies walking
through glass
to be ignored, never
picked out

no books to be read
yet they stack and stack
"maybe later"
as feeds scroll by & by & by

A productivity killer
A depression exacerbator
An anxiety fueler

dreams tick by, die
cat memes

political discord
digression in intelligence

This phone deconstructs the fabric of me
countless, endless
lack of self-control-less ways

an umbilical cord, tethered
a never-ending server
false dopamine booster
narrative through daily cycle

no boredom
no genius

no boredom
no genius

keep scrolling through,
we've reached critical mass

The Injustices I See

You stomp
and blather
roll lies from tongues
so corrupted
like you use meth for toothpaste

Your sticky cabbage hands
stomp through our halls
of democracy
swinging flags of failed rebellions
opposing all we think we've stood for

Generations have sat
curled up on the lawn
in front of forefathers
and spoken words of freedom

You stomp
and blather
roll lies from tongues
you have been taught are truths

Unable to see the history
leading you to
the desecration
of colonized ideals laid
before us by Greek
philosophers

But who am I to name
the injustices I see?
Who am I to cry to the
wind and hope?

That these are death throes
of ways we should long,
long be past

Death throes
that surprise me
yet don't

I have no voice in these truths
no voice to stomp
putting out fires that smolder for centuries

Yet here I am
small, intimidated
using a voice that's new to me

I'll be louder
I'll cry off canyons, let the wind
whip my words
nestling them in all four corners
of the earth.

You stomp
roll lies from tongues
so corrupted

yet we will bloom around your
blathering desecration
BLOOM around it
spread like wild weeds
through prairie
desert and ocean
single buds on the highest of our mountains
through your anarchy,

my voice will sing in a chorus with others
to fix what's always been broken
stomp our walls
and borders
my blood will mingle with theirs
not yours
and we will bleed to fix the world.

The sun stays longer

illuminating sky
rays seeping to
the glittering white
of ground,

feeling spring
though not close
breeding a false divine
to skins missing sun-kissed bliss.

Days lengthening
leaning into a bravado
that tricks the eye
singing flowers wish to bloom.

A smothering blanket
keeping them nestled
tight to ground.

Mouth wishing for
dandelion kisses
a chapping from
the sun and wind,

carrying stories
of stoic mountain men
stripping their breaks
and moccasins,

maidens' hair left loose
a swirling of freckles
sun warming.

Days lengthen
sunsets happen later,
a winter-wornness giving open

to thoughts of
life that stirs through us,
as bees dance through languid
honeyed moments.

Bare feet trod
on rebirthed greenness
of goddesses,

dreams of summer
living in fabric that keep us
stitched together
warming.

As midwinter's sun
tricks the divining
that stretches out upon days,

wishing for a melt
a summer blazing.

The bees, and their flowered partners
sleeping upon the snowbound
hidden gems of sprouting seedlings,

with atoms buzzing
in anticipation of lengthened winter
days, stretching their tips
toward summer.

Victor, Idaho, February 2021.

Bones sticking through

In my dreams
I dream of a world
where flags fly rainbows
instead of swastikas

For rainbows become us all
and swastikas breed death
on cold ground

Where the ancestors sleep
in mass graves
huddled together
bones sticking through
where skin had never been

Rainbows sing of love
a light that encompasses
everything that lives

Flowers, grass, and man

Where rainbow
colors bleed together
creating their own shades of love

For woman and child
a safety
that this world has
yet to know

In my reality, I see
swastikas
emblazoned on American flags

I fear for my children
who have yet to feel the touch,
of that violent burning temple

Left here in embers
while flames are reunited
licking up the sides
of gravestones

bearing marks
of ancestors huddled together
fingers bleeding
from barbed wire fences
bones sticking through
where skin has never been.

In my dreams
I dream of a world
where flags fly rainbows
and swastikas have been long buried

A safety, for every woman
and child
love blurring rainbow lines into one.

I dream of sitting in movie theaters

popcorn butter dripping off my fingers

holding a too-big soda

darkness blankets us

like we lay in one large

uncomfortable bed

When the lights go down

a hush falls like a wave from

back to front

every face turns slightly up

for stories that feel like an escape

yet so real

balms for the weary soul

The speakers reverberate

each person becomes the same shadow

connected in a shared stranger experience

forgetting the uncomfortableness of the bed we share

Swept, free of earthly needs,

earthly worries, earthly responsibilities

Cars drive fast, banks are robbed

lovers meet in darkened alleyways

we feel their souls, not as made-up spectators

as ourselves

delved deep into wishes, moments that speak to

us, the fabric that makes us

I dream of sitting in a movie theater

slightly sticky floors

wishing of the places they take us

the nearness of our lovers

the tears and laughter shared with a best friend

Popcorn butter dripping off my fingers

Damp earth smelling

of mud and rock
fresh new life that
springs from the depths
of its winter blanket

A dying season drips
from roof edge, tree branch
cascading into the frozen dirt
reviving what's been lost
from a year ago

Pools of lost dreams
puddle in the freshly curated
silt of what's to come
from a bipolar mother who
melts us one day

And tries to tuck us back into
the cocoon of cozy, yet
freezing coverings
only to have them both become
the fabric that breathes light back

Into us, while the sun stays steady
holy, arms outstretched to

welcome our upturned faces
breathing spring into our petals
like flowers that sway in breezes

We haven't met yet, petals that are
so new, so fragile, that warm breath
that ruffles them could either break or
exhale, profound spring life back into
the depths of us.

I search
and I search

for the ties to a land

my white ancestors stole

from indigenous people

I search

and search

to find MY indigenous roots

my tie to the lands that swell

rich with ancestral history

Only to find

Christianity spread through

Viking land

killing my pagan roots

Only to find

my people, pushed from Jerusalem

cattle hoarded on train cars

murdered in gas chambers

buried in unmarked graves

I search

and I search

for an ancestral connection

displaced by immigration

to lands that don't belong to me

To find

Christianity spread out

and killed the earth here too

It started

with Roman conquest

but it didn't end there
It spread
 and spread
Boot by boot
 only to find hold
  in traditions stolen
     from my pagan mothers
      your barbarian fathers
I've searched
 and I searched
  for an identity
   I never had
That Slav
 That Norse
  That Celt
   That Jew
Had burned out
 of every stolen tradition
    forced to follow, boat by boat
To come to lands
 seeking a freedom
  stolen
  with infected blankets
Only for me
 to never know
  of where my ties
   to this land
    come from
     displaced, and never home.

I search
and search
for soil that gives me comfort
dirt my ancestors walked
rocks that speak languages I've lost
from nomadic ancestors
escaping the ties that bound them
leaving generations of
immigrants, lost without roots.

There have been many definitions of me

Daughter, Sister, Writer, Delinquent, Healer, Lover, Wife

Mother

Mother

Definitions have been plagues upon my soul

As the nest empties
one by lonely one

I must redefine myself
examine each new day

Nothing has been so different, yet
the same all at once

Where I end, and
others begin

Where others end, and
I begin

There has been loss
belly laughter, love
tears stained my face
an ever-evolving path

a collective consciousness

A purpose is all that matters
where the dirty dishes lead to
a voice that wants to
speak so loudly
the world can hear it sing

But WHO am I?
What defines me?

Is it this sea of responsibility?
I thought life would quiet
as the babies flew
instead, it's grown before me
deafening, silent

Is it a moment staring at the ceiling?
hoping the moment lasts
hand pressed to my chest
a whisper at the cracks
"Just a little longer"
"Just a minute more"

No different now
than when the toddler
pulled at my presence

When is it escaping to the distant worlds?

Woven throughout the books
lining abandoned bookshelves
succumbing to musical notes that
reverberate into whirly nebulas
a stolen minute to write my soul
stitched to paper
like a messy field dressing
bandages for others to devour

A redefining of self
from daily mothering
to a confining freedom of a feather
drifting nest

WHO am I?
WHAT am I?

The definitions of me
that could disappear
under covers of a long-forgotten bed

Yet in these moments
the quiet ones
the still ones

I'm reminded of
the beauty of the life
I built
the joy that comes after

the struggle
the laugh lines around
my eyes

That, even in the coldest months
this home feels like summer's brightest breeze
but, mostly
I'm reminded of
who I've always been
who I'll always be
Daughter, Sister, Writer, Delinquent, Healer, Lover, Wife, Poet

Afterword

In June of 2020, my father was diagnosed with stage IV metastatic bladder cancer. It started as something we thought could be treated, but quickly turned into a whirlwind of crazier and crazier diagnoses. Then he was hospitalized after an emergency brain surgery to remove a tumor in his frontal lobe, in the hope that radiation could save his life. What we didn't know was that just three weeks later, on August 2, he would pass away in the early morning hours without any of us there with him because of COVID restrictions.

This book first started as a way for me to process how fast each of these events flew past me. I hadn't written a poem in almost two years. I reached out to a friend who had just gone through the same experience with her father. She also lost him to cancer. Knowing instinctively that my dad's time was almost up, I asked her if there were books or anything else that had helped her process this grief. Her response to me was, "I wrote. I wrote on napkins, receipts in my purse, anything I could find, I wrote everything down." And so, I wrote everything down. Furiously. Tears blurring every word. Rage climbing out of me. I WROTE it all.

Strangely, this is some of the best poetry I've ever written. It's raw and full of emotion, capturing something I've tried to do with my poetry since middle school. I use nature, landscapes, and the senses as emotions, anger as fire, tears as the ocean, rivers, and lakes, and bare feet grounding to the soil on which we stand.

I never thought of myself as a POET, never. Poetry was always something I held close and used to journal. When things grew too big and I needed a place for them to go, I wrote poetry. My other writing was always my focus—articles, short stories, a memoir, and, hopefully, a novel. My father always encouraged me, "a gift," he'd tell me—a book was always my goal. I never even considered writing a book of poetry, but as I started sharing this very raw material with friends, and as my dad quickly declined, I birthed a dream of an entire book.

This volume was originally going to be a chapbook, focused solely on the death of my Pop and the journey of my grief and healing. But I quickly realized I couldn't dwell in the loss I felt. I couldn't sit in this space for months or years. My dad wouldn't want that, and my life wouldn't allow it. This book grew from a place of grief and who I am—the adult child, before and after the loss of a parent—an adult who deals with chronic depression and anxiety, yet has to maintain a balance between working and parenting in a pandemic, while still going through the process of loss.

This book is a journey from my childhood in the 1980s through my life now, in the 2020s. What if I hadn't plunged into this process? What if I'd not needed an outlet? Suppose I continued to use writer's block to excuse why nothing ever got onto the page. If I hadn't accepted my poetry and called myself a poet, this collection of work that I am immensely proud of would be living between the notes app on my phone and random notebooks. I would never have seen them all together in one manuscript. My message to you: write the damn thing!

The core section (the starting section) of this book was the section titled "Dad." I'm a heavy poet. I kept hoping I could get something lighter out of myself; I don't think I ever did, and that's okay. I hope you've found moments of inspiration, an understanding that we all go through hard things—that we aren't alone, even when we feel we are, and that my voice can be your voice. A reminder that, in those challenging moments, if you can steal away for just a minute to write that poem, that short story, or that thought on a napkin or gum wrapper that's floating around the bottom of your bag, do it. The poem "Vermilion" was written on the back of a bank receipt in the late '90s, while driving through the Vermilion Cliffs in Northern Arizona with my Pop. It's still one of the poems I've written that I love the most. That memory with my dad is everything. Later, when he drove through again, he collected a jar of dirt; remembering that trip, he gave it to me a few years ago for safekeeping when he was moving. If we don't capture the little things, the big things can drown us. Use the back of this book—I'm giving you pages for just this purpose—to write when you are inspired.

I hope you enjoyed my journey of a lonely child with a wild imagination. To a teenage runaway. To a very settled wife and mother living in the mountains, writing my life away. To a child who lost her dad and wasn't sure how she'd survive that loss, but she did, and the deeper exploration of self, and who we are, before and after each big life transition.

Bio

Born in 1978 to parents finding their way through the Los Angeles music business, Adanna's life has constantly been submerged in art. Moving to upstate New York at a young age, she attended a Waldorf/Steiner school on a small, working organic dairy farm. An unconventional education provided a start in her journey of writing and painting. Waldorf education also provided a lifelong acceptance of her creative mind and the depths to which her imagination could take her. With dreams of being a travel journalist and novelist as a child, and a vision of filling others' lives with stories and beauty, Adanna wove her way through many different careers to finally land where she always knew she should be. After a fifteen-year nursing career to a hairstylist to today, where she works as a literary publicist and web designer, Adanna makes sure her entire world revolves around literature. Adanna writes about life inspired by nature and has a deep desire to make the world a better place, one word at a time. *Threadbare* is her first book of poetry. She lives with her husband, stepsons, and daughter in the mountains of Idaho.

Photo: Teton Canyon, Alta, Wyoming, August 4, 2012.

NOTES

CPSIA information can be obtained
at www.ICGtesting.com
Printed in the USA
FSHW011110250122
87650FS

9 781737 691679